F.R.I.E.N.D.S.H.I.P.

Space for Personalized Message

Friendship: A Poem of Appreciation

ACRONYM POETRY GIFT SERIES

By Macarena Luz Bianchi

Illustrated by Zonia Iqbal

To receive a free ebook, exclusive content, more wonder, wellness, and wisdom, sign up for her *Lighthearted Living* e-newsletter at MacarenaLuzB.com and check out her other poems of self-expression, books, and projects.

ISBN: Hardcover: 978-1-954489-11-0 | Paperback: 978-1-954489-12-7 | Ebook: 978-1-954489-13-4

Imprint

Spark Social, Inc. Miami, FL, USA, SparkSocialPress.com

Ordering Information: Licensing, custom books, and special discounts are available on quantity purchases. For details, contact the publisher at info@sparksocialpress.com.

F.R.I.E.N.D.S.H.I.P.

A Poem of Appreciation

ACRONYM POETRY GIFT SERIES

Macarena Luz Bianchi

Imprint
Spark Social Press

Friends for life in a solid friendship of fun! We chillax, are silly, and lift each other up.

Reveling rebels, seen and understood, no matter what.

Immediately available with
indispensable smiles.

Encouraging and supportive with empowering advice.

Nourishing conversations we can count on for a nudge or a laugh.

Delightfully trusting, what a fantastic friendship to have!

Sanctuary for nonsense and camaraderie.

Happy and healthy with
leeway and liberty.

Inseparable and connected regardless of distance, time, and space.

Pleased and proud of our genuine friendship. I appreciate you are my confidant, my cohort, my friend.

F.R.I.E.N.D.S.H.I.P.
A POEM OF APPRECIATION

Friends for life in a solid friendship of fun! We chillax, are silly, and lift each other up.

Reveling rebels, seen and understood, no matter what.

Immediately available with indispensable smiles.

Encouraging and supportive with empowering advice.

Nourishing conversations we can count on for a nudge or a laugh.

Delightfully trusting, what a fantastic friendship to have!

Sanctuary for nonsense and camaraderie.

Happy and healthy with leeway and liberty.

Inseparable and connected regardless of distance, time, and space.

Pleased and proud of our genuine friendship. I appreciate you are my confidant, my cohort, my friend.

৩ে৩৩৩

Thank you, Dear Reader!

Get Inspired & Stay Connected

To receive a free ebook, exclusive content, more wonder, wellness, and wisdom, sign up for her Lighthearted Living e-newsletter at MacarenaLuzB.com and check out her other poems of self-expression, books, and projects. ✨

Your Feedback is Appreciated

If you like this book, please review it to help others discover it. If you have any other feedback, please let us know at info@macarenaluzb.com or via the contact page at MacarenaLuzB.com. We would love to hear from you and know which topics you want in the next books. 💁

About the Author

Macarena Luz Bianchi has a lighthearted and empowering approach and is affectionally considered a Fairy Godmother by her readers. Beyond her collection of gift books and poems, she writes screenplays, fiction, and non-fiction for adults and children. She loves tea, flowers, and travel.

Subscribe to her *Lighthearted Living* newsletter for a free ebook and exclusive content at MacarenaLuzB.com and follow her on social media. 💖

Macarena Luz Bianchi

Gift Book Series

ACRONYM POETRY COLLECTION

- *Anniversary: A Poem of Affection*
- *Be My Valentine: A Poem of Love*
- *Congratulations: A Poem of Triumph*
- *Happy Birthday: A Poem of Celebration*
- *Intimacy: A Poem of Adoration*
- *Sympathy: A Poem of Solace*

With more to come including: *Encouragement, Graduation,* and so on.

POETRY COLLECTION

- *Glorious Mom: A Poem of Appreciation*
- *Gratitude Is: A Poem of Empowerment*
- *Gratitude Is: Poem & Coloring Book*
- *The Grateful Giraffes: What is Gratitude?*

Also available for children and in Spanish: Colección de Poesía I.